REVELATION

THE TRIUMPH
OF CHRIST

12 STUDIES WITH COMMENTARY

FOR INDIVIDUALS OR GROUPS

JOHN STOTT *BIBLE STUDIES*

JOHN STOTT

WITH DALE LARSEN
AND SANDY LARSEN

An imprint of InterVarsity Press
Downers Grove, Illinois

InterVarsity Press, USA
P.O. Box 1400
Downers Grove, IL 60515-1426, USA
ivpress.com
email@ivpress.com

Inter-Varsity Press, England
36 Causton Street
London SW1P 4ST, England
ivpbooks.com
ivp@ivpbooks.com

InterVarsity Press® is the book-publishing division of InterVarsity Christian Fellowship/USA®, a movement of students and faculty active on campus at hundreds of universities, colleges, and schools of nursing in the United States of America, and a member movement of the International Fellowship of Evangelical Students. For information about local and regional activities, visit intervarsity.org.

Inter-Varsity Press, England, originated within the Inter-Varsity Fellowship, now the Universities and Colleges Christian Fellowship, a student movement connecting Christian Unions in universities and colleges throughout Great Britain, and a member movement of the International Fellowship of Evangelical Students. That historic association is maintained, and all senior IVP staff and committee members subscribe to the UCCF Basis of Faith. Website: www.uccf.org.uk.

This study guide is based on and includes excerpts adapted from The Incomparable Christ ©2001 by John R. W. Stott.

Cover design and image composite: Cindy Kiple
Interior design: Daniel van Loon
Images: dark blue abstract painting © oxygen / Moment Collection / Getty Images

ISBN 978-0-8308-2179-2 (print)
ISBN 978-0-8308-5598-8 (digital)

Printed in the United States of America ♾

P   25   24   23   22   21   20   19   18   17   16   15   14   13   12   11   10   9   8   7   6   5   4   3

Y   39   38   37   36   35   34   33   32   31   30   29   28   27   26   25   24

CONTENTS

INTRODUCING REVELATION

Readers' reactions to the book of Revelation are remarkably varied. Some Christians are obsessed with it. They suppose that, together with the apocalyptic chapters of the book of Daniel in the Old Testament, it contains a secret history of the world—especially of contemporary events and people—and that they have the key to decipher it.

Other Christians, far from becoming obsessed with Revelation, go to the opposite extreme of neglect. They know that the book contains much bizarre imagery. Readers are understandably mystified and even intimidated by these unfamiliar phenomena. So they shy away from the book, or if they begin, they quickly give up in despair.

A third and positive reaction is exemplified by Richard Bauckham, who is a scholar on the book of Revelation. He begins his study titled *The Climax of Prophecy* with these words: "The Apocalypse of John is a work of immense learning, astonishingly meticulous literary artistry, remarkable creative imagination, radical political critique, and profound theology" (*The Climax of Prophecy* [Edinburgh: T&T Clark, 1993], ix).

This expert's evaluation should encourage us to persevere—as should the special blessing that is promised in Revelation 1:3 to both the lector who reads the book in the public assembly and to those who hear the reading and take to heart what they hear (see Revelation 22:18-19).

HOW DO WE READ REVELATION?

As we begin studying this exciting and challenging book, let's consider four principles of interpretation.

First, *Revelation is full of symbolism*. There are probably two explanations. To begin with, John is handling transcendent truths that cannot be expressed in straightforward prose, and it would be not only impossible but imprudent for him to do so. John is writing about the refusal of Christians to worship the emperor and about the overthrow of the Roman Empire, which would have been regarded by the authorities as seditious. Further, the symbols in Revelation are to be understood, not visualized. If we were to attempt to visualize them, the result often would be grotesque.

Second, *Revelation addresses the past, the present, and the future.* Indeed these are the three classic theories of interpretation. The *preterist* view regards almost all of the book as alluding to the past. The *historicist* view reads the book as telling the story of the church stage by stage during the whole period between the first and second comings of Christ, including our own generation. The third or *futurist* view expects most of the book to be fulfilled immediately before the parousia (the second coming of Christ).

It is unnecessary to be forced to choose between these three, for God's Word is intended to speak to the church in every age. It seems better, therefore, to adopt a *parallelist* view, which sees every section of the book as recapitulating the whole "interadventual" period between the two comings of Christ, each concluding with a scene of judgment and salvation.

Third, *Revelation celebrates the victory of God.* It depicts conflict between God and Satan, the Lamb and the dragon, the church and the world, the bride and the harlot, the holy city Jerusalem and the great city Babylon, those marked on their foreheads with the name of Christ and those marked with the name of the beast. The book's perspective is that Christ has conquered already and that his people are meant to share in his victory.

Fourth, *Revelation focuses on Jesus Christ.* The first three words of the book's Greek text are, "*Apokalypsis Iēsou Christou*," that is, an apocalypse or revelation of Jesus Christ. The book is above all else an unveiling of the greatness and glory of Christ. For this is what a beleaguered and persecuted church needed more than anything else—not a series of prophecies about the past or the future, nor even a coded panorama of church history, but a disclosure of the incomparable Christ, once crucified, now resurrected and reigning, and one day returning in power and great glory.

SUGGESTIONS FOR INDIVIDUAL STUDY

1. As you begin each study, pray that God will speak to you through his Word.

2. Read the introduction to the study and respond to the question that follows it. This is designed to help you get into the theme of the study.

3. The studies are written in an inductive format designed to help you discover for yourself what Scripture is saying. Each study deals with a particular passage so that you can really delve into the author's meaning in that context. Read and reread the passage to be studied. The questions are written using the language of the New International Version, so you may wish to use that version of the Bible. The New Revised Standard Version is also recommended.

4. Each study includes three types of questions. *Observation* questions ask about the basic facts: who, what, when, where, and how. *Interpretation* questions delve into the meaning of the passage. *Application* questions (also found in the "Apply" section) help you discover the implications of the text for growing in Christ. These three keys unlock the treasures of Scripture.

   Write your answers to the study questions in the spaces provided or in a personal journal. Writing can bring clarity and deeper understanding of yourself and of God's Word.

5. In the studies you will find some commentary notes designed to give help with complex verses by giving further biblical and cultural background and contextual information. The notes in the studies are not designed to answer the questions for you. They are to help you along as you learn to study the Bible for yourself. After you have worked through the questions, you may want to read John Stott's book *The Incomparable Christ*, on which this guide is based. This will give you more information about the text.

6. Move to the "Apply" section. These questions will help you connect the key biblical themes to your own life. Putting the application into practice is one of the keys to growing in Christ.

7. Use the guidelines in the "Pray" section to focus on God, thanking him for what you have learned and praying about the applications that have come to mind.

SUGGESTIONS FOR MEMBERS OF A GROUP STUDY

1. Come to the study prepared. Follow the suggestions for individual study mentioned above. You will find that careful preparation will greatly enrich your time spent in group discussion.

2. Be willing to participate in the discussion. The leader of your group will not be lecturing. Instead, she or he will be encouraging the members of the group to discuss what they have learned. The leader will be asking the questions that are found in this guide.

3. Stick to the topic being discussed. Your answers should be based on the verses that are the focus of the discussion and not on outside authorities such as commentaries or speakers. These studies focus on a particular passage of Scripture. Only rarely should you refer to other portions of the Bible. This allows for everyone to participate on equal ground and for in-depth study.

4. Be sensitive to the other members of the group. Listen attentively when they describe what they have learned. You may be surprised by their insights! Each question assumes a variety of answers. Many questions do not have "right" answers, particularly questions that aim at meaning or application. Instead the questions push us to explore the passage more thoroughly.

   When possible, link what you say to the comments of others. Also be affirming whenever you can. This will encourage some of the more hesitant members of the group to participate.

5. Be careful not to dominate the discussion. We are sometimes so eager to express our thoughts that we leave too little opportunity for others to respond. By all means participate! But allow others to also.

6. Expect God to teach you through the passage being discussed and through the other members of the group. Pray that you will have an

enjoyable and profitable time together but also that as a result of the study you will find ways that you can take action individually and/or as a group.

7. It will be helpful for groups to follow a few basic guidelines. These guidelines, which you may wish to adapt to your situation, should be read at the beginning of the first session.

- Anything said in the group is considered confidential and will not be discussed outside the group unless specific permission is given to do so. We will provide time for each person present to talk if he or she feels comfortable doing so.

- We will talk about ourselves and our own situations, avoiding conversation about other people.

- We will listen attentively to each other.

- We will be very cautious about giving advice.

8. If you are the group leader, you will find additional suggestions for you at the back of the guide.

THE FIRST AND THE LAST AND THE LIVING ONE

It was a Sunday. John was in exile on the island of Patmos. And he was "in the Spirit" as the revealing and inspiring Spirit took hold of him. Then, before he saw the vision, he heard a voice. Loud and peremptory, like the blast of a trumpet, and evidently the voice of Christ himself, it commanded John to write down on a scroll what he was about to see and to send it to the seven churches of the Roman province of Asia.

OPEN

What is the most awe-inspiring sight you have ever seen?

STUDY

Read Revelation 1:1-8. What is remarkable about these opening eight verses is that in them John unselfconsciously and unsystematically alludes to every event in the saving career of Jesus and so to the essence of the apostolic gospel.

1. Think of this opening passage as a sort of cover letter for John's message to his readers. What is the prevailing mood established by the opening?

2. Where is the central focus of these verses?

3. What promises are stated or implied (vv. 1, 3, 7)?

Even in the opening salutation, which in most letters is merely a conventional formula, John manages to include a greeting from the Trinity. After this greeting comes a personal doxology to Christ, celebrating what he has done for us. Then this doxology is immediately followed by an acclamation, declaring that Christ is coming back. The introduction ends with a divine statement in which God repeats that he is the One "who is, and who was, and who is to come"—one who is both "the Alpha and the Omega" and "the Almighty."

4. *Read Revelation 1:9-20.* How does John explain his presence on the island of Patmos (v. 9)?

5. John's senses are suddenly overwhelmed by what he sees and hears. What aspects of the figure seem human?

6. What aspects of the figure seem beyond human?

7. What clues do you find to the identity of the figure?

8. What influences have formed your mental pictures of Christ?

John found his attention first caught by seven golden lampstands (v. 12). They are only the framework, however. Much more important is the person standing among them, in their midst. He is called someone "like a son of man," that is, resembling a human figure (an expression borrowed from Daniel 7 and 10, which supplies much of the description in verses 13-16).

9. Focus on verses 17-20. How does John react to the Person he sees?

10. How does the Person reassure him?

Summary: Not only did the vision cause John to fear but so did the whole situation in which he found himself. He was in exile. What did the future hold for him and for the Christian communities in Asia for which he was responsible? To a church enduring persecution and facing the possibility of martyrdom, Christ's message is more than the command "Do not be afraid." It is also the basis of Christian fearlessness. *First*, Christ shares the eternity of God. The title he claims, "I am the First and the Last" (Revelation 1:17), is virtually identical with God's claim, "I am the Alpha and the Omega" (Revelation 1:8). *Second*, he calls himself "the Living One," not in the sense that he survived death but that his dead body was resurrected and simultaneously transformed. So because Christ is both the Eternal One and the Resurrected One, death has lost its terror, and we have every reason to rejoice and not be afraid.

11. How does Christ express his victory over death (vv. 17-18)?

12. How does Christ explain the significance of the seven lampstands (v. 20)?

Summary: The first "revelation of Jesus Christ" is of the risen and eternal Christ. His resurrection is foundational. He is presented throughout, in spite of the onslaughts of the devil, as victorious, having won a decisive victory over evil by his death and resurrection.

APPLY

How does John's vision challenge your ideas of the risen Christ?

How can John's vision affect your worship?

What difference has it made for you to know that Christ is living and reigning now?

PRAY

What aspects of your life would change if you had full assurance that Christ is "the First and the Last" and "the Living One"? Pray about those areas of your life. Ask the Lord to bring to mind other people who need that same assurance, and pray for them.

THE SEVEN MARKS OF AN IDEAL CHURCH

The scene changes. Our vision is now focused not so much on the glorious human-divine figure of Christ as on the churches he walks among (Revelation 2:1). Since seven was the perfect or complete number (at least in the circles of the author and his readers), it seems legitimate to regard the seven individual churches of the province of Asia as together representing the universal church. And since one particular feature is emphasized in each church, we may perhaps regard these seven features as the marks of an ideal church.

OPEN

If you were to describe an ideal church, not the building but the people, what adjectives would you use?

What verbs would you use?

STUDY

All seven letters to the seven churches have an identical outline. First comes *an announcement* of both the recipient and the author of the letter. The author is, of course, Christ, but he describes himself differently in each letter. Second comes *an assertion*, which begins in each case with the two words "I know." Third, Christ sends each church *a message* adapted to their situation, for each is either praiseworthy or blameworthy. The fourth part of each letter is *an appeal*, always the same: "Whoever has ears, let them hear what the Spirit says to the churches." Finally, each letter concludes with *a promise* to Christian overcomers.

1. *Read Revelation 2:1-11.* Fill in the chart.

	ANNOUNCEMENT	ASSERTION	MESSAGE	PROMISE
Ephesus				
Smyrna				

2. *Read Revelation 2:12-29.* Fill in the chart.

	ANNOUNCEMENT	ASSERTION	MESSAGE	PROMISE
Pergamum				
Thyatira				

3. *Read Revelation 3:1-22.* Fill in the chart.

	ANNOUNCEMENT	ASSERTION	MESSAGE	PROMISE
Sardis				
Philadelphia				
Laodicea				

4. Taking chapters 2–3 as a whole, what are the sins for which Christ most strongly demands repentance?

5. What are the elements that Christ finds most praiseworthy in the churches of chapters 2–3?

6. Look back at the first line of each of the letters to the churches to see how Christ describes himself (2:1, 8, 12, 18; 3:1, 7, 14). What stands out to you about this list?

Summary: The risen Lord reveals himself as the chief pastor of his flock. Patrolling, inspecting, and supervising his churches, he has intimate knowledge of them and is able to pinpoint the seven marks that he would like every church to display: love for him, willingness to suffer for him, truth of doctrine, holiness of life, commitment to mission, sincerity, and wholeheartedness in everything. We also see the church hard-pressed by sin, error, and lethargy from within and by tribulation and persecution from without, especially by the temptation to forsake Christ for Caesar and by the real risks of martyrdom.

7. If Christ were speaking to your own church fellowship, where do you think he would call for your repentance?

8. What elements of your church fellowship do you think he would find most praiseworthy?

APPLY

How is Christ calling you to personal repentance?

What steps do you need to take to fulfill your repentance (for example, forgiving or seeking forgiveness)?

How can you confirm and make more habitual those ways you are faithfully obeying Christ?

PRAY

Pray for your church fellowship, that your life together will be more Christlike. Pray that your ears will be open to "hear what the Spirit says to the churches."

SHARING GOD'S THRONE

REVELATION 4-5

After this I looked, and there before me was a door standing open in heaven. And the voice I had first heard speaking to me like a trumpet said, 'Come up here, and I will show you what must take place after this'" (Revelation 4:1). It was the open door of revelation, and as John looked through the door, what he saw developed in three stages: first, a throne, from which God rules over the universe; second, a scroll—the book of history—closed, sealed, and held in God's right hand; and finally, a Lamb as slain, who alone is worthy to open the scroll, to interpret, and to control history.

OPEN

What does it mean to you that God is on a throne?

STUDY

It is significant that when John peeped through the open door, the very first thing he saw was a throne, the symbol of the sovereignty, majesty, and kingly rule of God. The churches of Asia were small and struggling; the might of Rome seemed invincible. Already the powers of darkness seemed to be closing in on them. Yet they need have no fear, for at the center of the universe stands a throne. Everything John saw in his vision was related to the throne.

1. *Read Revelation 4:1-11.* Although the scene is beyond human description, what features come through most strongly in John's attempt to describe what he saw?

2. Describe the scene of worship in verses 6-11.

3. How does the scene here compare with what is commonly regarded as worship?

4. How do you account for the difference?

Summary: We seize the assurances of the book of Revelation that one day there will be no more hunger or thirst, no more pain or tears, no more sin, death, or curse—for all these things will have passed away. It would be better and more biblical, however, to focus not so much on these absences as on the cause of their absence: the central, dominating presence of God's throne.

5. *Read Revelation 5:1-5.* Why did the scroll cause grief for John?

6. From what the elder told him, what would John expect to see next (v. 5)?

7. *Read Revelation 5:6-10.* What surprisingly bold action does the Lamb take (v. 7), and what is the reaction from those around him (vv. 8-10)?

John looked to see this triumphant lion, and to his astonishment, he saw instead a Lamb, looking as if it had been slaughtered yet standing in the very center of the throne, sharing it with God. Thus our attention is directed from the throne to the scroll and now from the scroll to the Lamb.

8. Why was the Lamb worthy to open the scroll (vv. 5, 9)?

9. Aside from the fact that Jesus is identified as the Lamb of God (John 1:29, 36), how else can you be sure that the Lamb seen by John is Jesus Christ?

10. *Read Revelation 5:11-14.* How does the praise of the Lamb now expand outward from the throne?

11. When have you felt that you were participating in worship along with all of God's creation? If you have never felt that way, what is the closest that you have experienced?

Summary: It is a magnificent vision of the whole creation on their faces before God and Christ, and it is truly amazing that the Lamb is bracketed with the occupant of the throne, sharing it with him and receiving equal praise. The cross illumines history because it speaks of victory, of redemption, and of suffering. At the center of God's throne, a symbol of power, stands a slain Lamb, a symbol of weakness. Power through weakness, dramatized in God on the cross and the Lamb on the throne, lies at the heart of ultimate reality, even the mystery of almighty God himself.

APPLY

When have you seen God work his power through weakness?

What does it say to you that the Lamb still appears wounded even on the throne?

What do the sufferings of the Lamb say about his love?

PRAY

Pray the prayers of Revelation 5:9-10 and 12-13 aloud. Add your own words of honor for Christ. Bring your most troublesome worries and concerns to him, and remember that you approach the all-powerful One who occupies the throne.

THE COURSE OF HISTORY

Having celebrated the Lamb's unique right to open the scroll, and having seen him take it from the throne occupant, John now watches as the Lamb breaks the seven seals one by one. After each of the first four is broken, one of the living creatures shouts in a voice like thunder, "Come!" and behold, a horse and its rider appears. These are the famous "four horsemen of the Apocalypse," well known to Christian artists.

OPEN

When a catastrophe strikes somewhere in the world, whether natural or caused by human action, many people immediately think of God. How do such events affect your ideas about God's sovereignty and God's love?

What do you pray at those times?

STUDY

1. *Read Revelation 6:1-8.* How do the appearances of the four horses and riders differ from each other?

2. What similarities do you see in the four horses and riders?

Because the rider on a white horse belongs to the series of apocalyptic horsemen, many commentators conclude that he, like the others, symbolizes disaster—in his case, military conquest. But throughout Revelation white stands for righteousness; crowns and conquest belong to Christ; and in Revelation 19:11-16 the rider on a white horse is named "Faithful and True," "the Word of God," and even "King of kings and Lord of lords." So we are assured that, before the other horsemen spread the horrors of war, famine, and death, Christ rides first at the head of the cavalcade, resolved to win the nations by the gospel. And he succeeds!

3. *Read Revelation 6:9-11.* The fifth seal reveals the souls of martyrs. What is their plea and the response?

4. What does the vision say to you about the relationship between the world and the Christian faith?

5. *Read Revelation 6:12-17.* This passage describes the most appalling cosmic convulsions. How are the great upheavals explained (vv. 16-17)?

Summary: This opening drama of the first six seals gives us a general overview of history between the first and second comings of Christ. It will be a time of violent disturbance and suffering, but the eye of faith looks beyond these things to Christ, who is both the crowned and conquering rider on the white horse and the Lamb who breaks the seals, controlling the course of history.

We now have to wait until Revelation 8:1 for the seventh seal to be broken. John treats us to an interlude that stresses the security of the people of God.

6. *Read Revelation 7:1-8.* What priority is given to the sealing or marking of the 144,000?

7. How are they identified (v. 3)?

8. *Read Revelation 7:9-12.* Who does John see next, and engaged in what actions?

9. Let yourself join in the songs of the multitude and the angels (vv. 10, 12). Read their words aloud. How do their words affect you?

Summary: Revelation 7 describes two human communities. The first numbers 144,000 and is drawn from the twelve tribes of Israel; the second is a huge, unnumbered multitude drawn from all nations, languages, and tribes. At first sight, they seem to be two distinct groups (numbered and unnumbered, Israel and Gentiles). But on closer inspection, it becomes clear that both are pictures of the same redeemed community of God, although viewed from different perspectives. In the first, the people are assembled like soldiers in battle array—the church militant on earth—and in the second they are assembled before God, their conflicts past—the church triumphant in heaven.

10. *Read Revelation 7:13-17.* What is the blessed state of the multitude in white robes?

11. How have they arrived at this state (v. 14)?

Summary: How can we make sure that we belong to this redeemed, international throng? We cannot possibly stand before God's dazzling throne in the soiled and tattered rags of our own morality but rather only if we have sought cleansing from the Lamb who died for us. Since all the redeemed are being described, the tribulation of verse 14 cannot refer to the specific period between the appearance of the antichrist and the parousia of Christ. It must be a description of the whole Christian life, which the New Testament repeatedly designates as a time of tribulation.

APPLY

What is the greatest test of faith that you face right now?

In Revelation 6–7 what specific encouragement in Christ do you find to help you meet that test?

PRAY

Consider the promises of Revelation 7:15-17 and the praise of Revelation 7:10, 12. Use the passages as a starting point for your own prayers of confidence and gratitude to the Lord.

CALLING THE WORLD TO REPENTANCE

REVELATION 8-9

In a dramatic entry into the next section of chapters (8–11), John describes an angel with a golden censer offering incense together with the prayers of God's people (Revelation 8:3-5). The smoke is ascending to the throne of God. Then there is a sudden change as the angel fills the censer with fire from the altar and hurls it to the earth. Thunder, lightening, and an earthquake follow. This divine reply of thunder and lightning, symbols of God's judgment, are in direct response to the church's prayers.

OPEN

When have you received a lifesaving warning?

What might have happened if you had ignored the warning?

STUDY

1. *Read Revelation 8:1-5.* What responses or questions do you have to the vision in verses 3-5?

2. How does this vision speak to you as you think about your own prayers?

Seven angels were given seven trumpets. It is important to remember, as the drama develops, that the breaking of the seven seals and the blowing of the seven trumpets are not consecutive but symbolize the same period, stretching between the two comings of Christ, although from different perspectives. What, then, is the distinctive perspective of the trumpets? What is its vision of Christ?

3. *Read Revelation 8:6-13.* The first four of seven angels sound their trumpets. What are the realms of the disasters that follow?

4. How is God's mercy shown even in the extent of the disasters?

Summary: The calamities listed (damage to the earth, sea, freshwater, and solar system) are not to be regarded as particular, let alone recognizable, events. If they are meant to be taken literally, then they contribute to the hazards of life on earth. But they are much more likely to be figurative and to allude to such happenings as environmental disaster (the green things of the first trumpet), economic chaos (the destroyed ships of the second), human tragedy (the bitterness of the third), and barbarian behavior (the darkness of the fourth). But the future will be even worse. The eagle cries,

"Woe! Woe! Woe!" to indicate that the fifth, sixth, and seventh trumpets will bring even more intense suffering and will, therefore, be renamed the first, second, and third woes.

5. If the first four trumpets described damage to nature, the fifth (Revelation 9:1-11) and sixth (Revelation 9:12-21) describe damage to human beings. *Read Revelation 9:1-12.* What is the origin of the terrible horde of locusts (vv. 1-3)?

6. The one thing locusts are known for—consuming swaths of vegetation—these creatures were expressly forbidden to do (v. 4). Instead they attacked the unbelieving world, which had not received God's seal. John's description of them is extremely vivid. Nine times he repeats the word *like*. To what does John compare their appearance and their power (vv. 3, 5, 7-10)?

These venomous creatures are not literal, nor does John give us any hint that they are demonic hordes. Is it possible, then, in light of Jesus' teaching that all kinds of evil lie buried in the human heart (Mark 7:21-23), that this is what John is graphically illustrating? The gospel reveals, to us and others, the deep depravity of our fallen nature. Often our fallen nature is hidden, but at times it breaks the surface, to our acute embarrassment. The gospel painfully convicts us of sin, for there is no pain more distressing than that of a tormented conscience. It leads some to repentance and faith, but it leads others to harden their hearts and so perish.

7. *Read Revelation 9:13-21.* John is aware that the sixth trumpet will bring even more acute suffering than any of the five previous ones. So he emphasizes that permission for it has come directly from God in answer to his people's prayers (see Revelation 8:3-5) and that it would

sound only at the exact moment that had been decreed by God (Revelation 9:15). What strikes you as most fearsome about the vision of Revelation 9:15-19?

8. What is God's intended purpose in the attacks (vv. 20-21)?

9. John records in his vision that those who survived death did not repent either of their idolatry (the worst breach of the first table of the law) or of their other sins (mostly those in breach of the second table). Why do you think people cling to certain sins so stubbornly?

10. What has God done to bring you to repentance for stubborn sins?

APPLY

Throughout Revelation 8–9, we see God going to extreme measures to call the world to repentance. What means do you think God is using in the world today to urge people to repent of sin?

What measures might God be taking in your own life to call you to repent of a particular sin?

PRAY

Ask the Holy Spirit to search your heart and reveal sin, especially those sins you have avoided admitting and facing. Accept his forgiveness purchased by Christ on the cross. Thank him for his mercy, and resolve to live in his continuing grace, no matter what your emotions may say to you.

REVEALING CHRIST'S GOSPEL TO THE WORLD

REVELATION 10-11

W e can now understand the seals, trumpets, and bowls as relating to the same period between Christ's comings but from different points of view. The seven seals describe what Christ *allows* in his world (since things happen only when he breaks the seals). The seven bowls (still to come) describe how Christ *judges* his world. But the seven trumpets (which come between the seals and the bowls) describe how Christ *warns* the world and summons them to repentance.

OPEN

Do you tend to associate the gospel message with power or with humility? Why?

STUDY

1. Between the sixth and seventh trumpets there is an interlude. *Read Revelation 10:1-7.* What are the actions and words of this astounding figure?

2. What clues do you get that the "mighty angel" has the authority of God?

As John describes his vision of "another mighty angel coming down from heaven" (v. 1), it is evident that this is no mere angel. Why should it not be the "angel of the Lord," who appeared in the Old Testament theophanies that seem to have been preincarnate appearances of the Son of God? John seems to have deliberately assembled a number of divine features in his description. The evidence seems overwhelming that this is Jesus Christ.

3. *Read Revelation 10:8-11.* John's attention is turned from the majestic angel to the little scroll in the angel's hand. What is John instructed to do and with what results?

4. Before John, Jeremiah and Ezekiel both had similar experiences with a scroll (Jeremiah 15:16; Ezekiel 3:1-3). Imagine, if possible, that you are John taking the action of Revelation 10:9. What is going through your mind as you approach the mighty angel with your request?

Summary: John was recommissioned to take the gospel to all nations (Mark 13:10) but was, at the same time, warned that the sweetness of the message of salvation would be followed by the bitterness of judgment for those who rejected God's Word.

5. John is instructed to measure the temple of God and the altar and to count the worshipers there (Revelation 11:1). Suddenly in Revelation 11:3, "two witnesses" are introduced. *Read Revelation 11:1-6.* What is the mission of the two witnesses (v. 3)?

6. What authority is given to the two witnesses (vv. 5-6)?

7. *Read Revelation 11:7-13.* When the two witnesses' testimony is finished, an unidentified beast from the Abyss, perhaps antichrist, will attack, overpower, and kill them (vv. 7-10). How are the two witnesses to be vindicated in the sight of their enemies (vv. 11-12)?

Summary: After a short period, the martyred and silenced church will be resurrected by God (its testimony revived), causing terror in the watching world, and it finally will be exalted to heaven, to the consternation of its enemies. This will be accompanied by a severe earthquake, spreading terror among the survivors. The nations will give glory to God, some by conversion, others by submission on the Day of Judgment.

8. *Read Revelation 11:14-19.* Although "the third woe is coming soon" (v. 14), the mood of the writing abruptly changes. Loud voices in heaven plus the voices of the twenty-four elders make great announcements in the form of praise to God. What *has happened* to cause them to rejoice (vv. 15-18)?

The verb tenses of Revelation 11:15-19 all indicate what has irrevocably taken place. All these statements attest to the finality of what has happened, either concluding the past or inaugurating the future.

9. How do the people of God take part in the victory of God (vv. 17-18)?

10. What significance do you find in God's temple being opened to reveal the ark of his covenant?

Summary: Now that the world has largely rejected the negative message of warning, much as Pharaoh had hardened his heart and refused to repent, the positive proclamation of the gospel is even more essential. For Christ is still calling the world to himself; his patience is not exhausted, and the end has not yet arrived.

APPLY

If the glorified Christ appears as described in Revelation 10:1-3, what gives you the courage to approach him in prayer?

Christ has already taken his kingdom and will reign forever. What parts of Revelation 11:15-18 stir you most deeply?

PRAY

Bring every troublesome element of your life to Christ. For each problem, make the bold prayer "Jesus, I know you are Lord over _____." Surrender each problem to him to deal with in his power and his time.

CHRIST OVERCOMING THE DEVIL AND HIS ALLIES

REVELATION 12–13

J ohn has again brought us full circle from the beginning to the conclusion of the gospel era, and with Revelation 12:1, the whole cycle will begin again. Each time that John recapitulates his story, as it stretches from Christ's first coming to his second, there is persecution, conflict, victory, and celebration.

OPEN

Throughout history Christians have been persecuted in one form or another, to one degree or another. Why do you think Christianity consistently draws persecution?

STUDY

1. In the opening vision of Revelation 12 there are three chief actors: a pregnant woman entering labor, the male child she bears, and an enormous red dragon with seven crowned heads and ten horns

symbolizing his powerful empire. *Read Revelation 12:1-6.* What remarkable series of events takes place?

2. What are the clues that the child who is born must be Christ (v. 5)?

There is no doubt about the identity of the dragon, since John refers to him in Revelation 12:9 as "that ancient serpent called the devil, or Satan." Nor is there any question about the male child; he is the Messiah, the King of kings (see Psalm 2:9). But who is the mother who gives birth to her son? The strongest hint occurs in Revelation 12:1, which reminds us of Joseph's dream in Genesis 37:9. This glorious lady, who gave birth to the Messiah, is a symbol of the people of Israel, from whose twelve patriarchs the human ancestry of the Christ is traced (Romans 9:5).

Summary: The first vision—of the woman, the child, and the dragon—is a marvelous condensation of the gospel story from the Messiah's birth in fulfillment of the Old Testament to his resurrection and ascension and on to the time of the persecution and protection of the church. It is also an expression of the age-long "enmity" between the serpent and the woman (Genesis 3:15).

3. *Read Revelation 12:7-17.* What is the outcome of the war in heaven (vv. 7-9)?

4. How does the voice in heaven pronounce both victory and warning (vv. 10-12)?

5. Although Christ's victory was achieved once for all on the cross, God's people have been given a way to enter into it themselves. How do believers share in the defeat of Satan (v. 11)?

Summary: At the cross Christ decisively vanquished the devil, and at the resurrection his victory was vindicated. What have now "come," and so become available to us, are "salvation" (for which Christ died), "power" (the gospel being God's power for salvation), "the kingdom of our God" (which broke into history through Christ), and "the authority of his Messiah" (who said that universal authority now belonged to him). These blessings are now ours because Satan the accuser has been overthrown.

6. *Read Revelation 12:13-17.* How does the dragon continue to relentlessly pursue the woman and with what results?

While the woman who gives birth to the child symbolizes the Old Testament people of God, the woman who is pursued by the devil symbolizes the New Testament people of God. There is an essential continuity between them. She flees into the desert—a new exodus—where she is cared for by God. So the devil becomes enraged and goes off to make war against the rest of her offspring, that is, the church of later generations, whose members obey God's commandments and faithfully bear witness to Jesus (v. 17). Obedience and testimony are two essential marks of the messianic community.

Summary: The dominant theme of chapter 12 is the decisive overthrow of the devil. He is foiled in his resolve to devour the Christ-child, who instead is snatched up to God. He is foiled in his engagement in spiritual warfare and instead is hurled down to the earth. He is foiled in his attempts to destroy the woman, who instead is rescued by God.

7. Like a diabolical parody of the Trinity, three allies of Satan will appear: "the beast out of the sea," "the beast out of the earth," and the gaudy prostitute "Babylon" (to be introduced in chapter 14). They all represent the city and empire of Rome, although from three different perspectives. *Read Revelation 13:1-10.* What powers are wielded by the beast out of the sea?

The Jews were always afraid of the sea. It seemed to them a continuation of the primeval chaos and even a symbol of hostility to God. The raging of the nations was like the raging of the sea (Isaiah 17:12). So a monster emerging out of the sea would be a particular horror.

8. How are believers radically different from those who worship the beast from the sea (vv. 8-10)?

9. *Read Revelation 13:11-18.* The beast out of the earth has no independent role. How does this second beast serve as a henchman for the first beast?

Although Revelation 13:14-15 must include all idolatry or worship of God substitutes, the most direct allusion is to the imperial cult—which is mentioned as having set up an image in honor of the beast, and the death penalty was applied to those who refused to worship it.

10. Keeping in mind that the second beast is subservient to the first beast (v. 12) and the first beast is subservient to the dragon/serpent/ Satan (Revelation 13:2), what does Revelation 12–13 tell you about Satan's strategies?

11. What do Revelation 12–13 tell you about the resources that believers have in Christ?

APPLY

This Scripture issues a challenge to God's people to endure, to be faithful, and to refuse to compromise. In extended times of testing, what has given you the ability to endure?

Consider a time when you would have to admit that you were unfaithful to the Lord. What brought you back to renew your faithfulness? Consider the influence of Scripture, other people's words, memories, the Holy Spirit's prompting, God-arranged circumstances, or other influences.

Where are you now tempted to compromise with the unbelieving world?

What have you found in Revelation 12–13 that strengthens your resistance to compromise with the world?

PRAY

Thank God that you can be among the overcomers (Revelation 12:11). Pray for endurance, faithfulness, and the courage to refuse to compromise with sin. Make your prayers as specific as possible.

CHRIST STANDING ON MOUNT ZION

REVELATION 14:1–15:4

John now gives us another of his welcome interludes. It would be hard to conceive of a sharper contrast than the one he depicts between Revelation chapters 13 and 14. It is an immense relief to turn from the dragon and his first beast, whose habitat is the unruly sea, to the Lamb who stands on firm and holy ground; from persecution and the threat of martyrdom to security in Mount Zion; from the incompleteness of 666 to the completeness of 144,000; and from those who have received the mark of the beast on their foreheads to those who have the name of the Lamb and of his Father written on their foreheads.

OPEN

Why is the reaping of a harvest a good metaphor for judgment?

STUDY

1. *Read Revelation 14:1-5*. Describe the extraordinary scene that John is witnessing. What does he see and hear?

2. In addition to the orchestra, there is a choir of 144,000. What are the distinguishing features of the singers (vv. 1, 3-5)?

3. The Lamb is named three times in this passage (vv. 1, 4). What does each occurrence say to you about his relationship with the redeemed throng?

4. *Read Revelation 14:6-13.* While the three angels have different messages, how do all three announce God's judgment?

5. How should God's people react to the announcements of judgment (v. 12)?

Summary: God's people are assured of final vindication. If they "die in the Lord," whether in martyrdom or by natural causes, they are truly "blessed" (v. 13). For they will rest from their labor, in contrast to the wicked, for whom there will be "no rest" (v. 11). Moreover, their deeds will follow them and give evidence of their loyalty.

6. The next passage divides the final judgment into two parts. *Read Revelation 14:14-20.* How does John describe the first figure who appears (v. 14)?

7. The figure reaps the harvest of earth (v. 16). What is the origin of the command to reap (v. 15)?

8. Next an angel appears to reap a second harvest. How does the second harvest differ from the first (vv. 17-20)?

The first reaper is surely the Lord Christ at his second coming. He wielded his sickle, "and the earth was harvested." We can only assume, therefore, that the first harvest is a grain harvest and represents the ingathering of the believing righteous. The second harvest is of grapes and concludes with the grapes being thrown into "the great winepress of God's wrath" (v. 19).

9. *Read Revelation 15:1-4.* After the terrible picture of judgment in Revelation 14, how does the scene dramatically change?

10. What is the defining feature of the seven last plagues (v. 1)?

11. Who are the singers by the "sea of glass glowing with fire" (v. 2)?

12. What is the theme of the song of Moses and the Lamb (vv. 3-4)?

Before John describes the outpouring of the seven bowls of God's wrath, which will be reminiscent of the plagues of Egypt, he draws a striking analogy between Israel's exodus from Egypt and the redemption achieved by Christ. Like the Israelites gathered by the Red Sea, victorious over Pharaoh, a multitude of people stand by what looks like a sea of glass and fire, victorious over the beast and his image. The song of Moses (the Old Testament victor) has become the song of the Lamb (the New Testament victor), praising God for the greatness of his deeds and the justice of his ways.

Summary: We cannot fail to be impressed that the incomparable Christ is at the center of each of John's visions. At the beginning of Revelation 14, we see him as the Lamb standing on Mount Zion, while at the end of the chapter we see him sitting on a cloud as the Son of Man with his sickle. In the former vision, he guarantees the security of his redeemed people; in the latter, he functions as a judge on the last day, separating the wheat from the chaff.

APPLY

When you consider the judgment of God, do you feel fearful? confident? mystified? some other emotion?

Look again at the descriptions of the redeemed (Revelation 14:1-5, 13; 15:2). What gives you the security that you are included in that multitude?

PRAY

Pray the song of Moses and the Lamb (Revelation 15:3-4). Thank God for the specific "righteous acts" you have seen him perform in your life and the lives of others.

LIKE A THIEF IN THE NIGHT

John saw "seven angels with the seven last plagues—last, because with them God's wrath is completed" (Revelation 15:1). We will see that after the outpouring of the seventh bowl, a loud voice from God's throne cries out, "It is done!" (Revelation 16:17). *Completed* and *done*. These are the two significant and telltale words. The previous judgments—the seals and the trumpets—were partial; those of the bowls are final.

OPEN

What reasons can you think of that God's judgment would cause rejoicing?

STUDY

Read Revelation 15:5–16:15. John sees in heaven that the temple stands open. That is, it is by the direct sanction of God that the seven angels emerge as agents of judgment. Their seven bowls are filled with the wrath of God, and the temple is full of God's glory so that no one can enter it until the judgment is over.

1. What do you think Jesus' "blessed" promise in Revelation 16:15 means in practical terms for a believer's life?

Jesus used the *thief* simile during his public ministry (Matthew 24:42-44; Luke 12:39-40). If only the thief would oblige us by sending us an advance notice, alerting us to the day and time of his intended visit! Then we would be ready. But no, his coming will be sudden and unexpected. Jesus' words to Sardis, "I will come like a thief" (Revelation 3:3), may have been a warning that he was coming to deal with the church's affairs. But in Revelation 16:15, he is surely referring to his second coming.

2. *Read Revelation 16:16-21.* John returns to the gathering of the kings and to their rendezvous at a place called in Hebrew *Armageddon.* What are the results of the catastrophic earthquake?

Many believe the name *Armageddon* to be derived from *Megiddo*, a strategic site in northern Palestine and the scene of many ancient battles. It is not literal, however. It symbolizes the final battle between the Lamb and the dragon, between Christ and antichrist. For Christ will come in power and glory to rout and destroy the forces of evil.

3. So far "Babylon" has been mentioned twice, in Revelation 14:8 and Revelation 16:19. Both verses refer to her overthrow under the judgment of God, but neither tells us what she symbolizes. Now two whole chapters are devoted to the phenomenon of "Babylon." Revelation 17 identifies her for us, while Revelation 18 describes in the most graphic detail her devastation and destruction. *Read Revelation 17:1-18.* What imagery does John use to describe the prostitute's immoral excesses (vv. 1-6)?

4. How has the great prostitute corrupted the earth (vv. 2-5)?

5. How has she persecuted Christian believers (v. 6)?

6. The scarlet beast the woman rides on is readily recognizable as the beast from the sea (Revelation 13:1). What does the angel say about the fate of the beast (vv. 7-8)?

The four stages in the biography of the beast may well be an allusion to Nero. According to a popular myth, Nero once was, now is not (he committed suicide), will rise again (either literally at the head of an army or symbolically in the policies of Domitian) but will be destroyed. This is also the course of evil—active from the beginning, seeming sometimes to die down, reasserting itself but ultimately to be destroyed.

Summary: The beast's seven heads are "seven hills on which the woman sits" (v. 9), those on which Rome is built. The woman is "the great city that rules over the kings of the earth" (v. 18), Babylon in symbol, Rome in reality—the very essence of hostility to Christ and his church.

7. Now that the identity of "Babylon" has been established as Rome—the prostitute, aided and abetted by Rome the persecutor—John goes on at once to describe her overthrow. It would not take place in its finality for more than another 320 years. Yet John uses the prophetic past tense throughout Revelation 18, expressing the certainty of God's judgment as if it had already taken place. *Read Revelation 18:1-24.* What reasons are given for Babylon's destruction (vv. 4-8)?

8. How are God's people vindicated by the destruction of Babylon (vv. 20, 24)?

9. What everyday, and even innocent, pursuits will cease in Babylon's destruction (vv. 11-23)?

Summary: In the first century AD Babylon was Rome. But Babylon has flourished throughout history and throughout the world. Its profile can be drawn with ease from these chapters. It seems to have six components: idolatry; immorality; extravagance and luxury; the use of sorcery and magic; tyranny and oppression, leading to the martyrdom of God's people; and arrogance, even self-deification. The urgent call still comes to God's people to come out of her, in order to avoid contamination (v. 4).

10. In contrast to the silence of burned-out Babylon, John now hears an overwhelming sound in heaven. *Read Revelation 19:1-10.* Five times *Hallelujah!*—that is, "Praise the Lord!"—is repeated, if the invitation to "praise our God" in Revelation 19:5 is included. As in the Psalms, *hallelujah* never stands alone. Always some reasons are added to explain why we should praise God. What are the reasons given here?

11. The wedding of the Lamb has come (v. 7)! How is the bride of the Lamb put in dramatic contrast to the great prostitute (vv. 7-9)?

Summary: We remember the gaudy clothing of the prostitute; by contrast, the bride prepared herself with simple "fine linen, bright and clean," which had been given to her to wear. The fine linen stands for the "righteous acts" of God's people, John adds. Without these she would not be fit for her bridegroom.

APPLY

These chapters of Revelation are filled with images from the most horrifying to the most exultant. What do they say to you about sin?

What do they say to you about heaven?

When you think of Christ coming like a thief in the night, how well prepared are you for his coming?

PRAY

Believers have the right to join in the repeated hallelujahs of Revelation 19. Praise God and thank him for his righteous judgment and that sin will be at last overthrown and ended.

CHRIST RIDING IN TRIUMPH

REVELATION 19:11–20:15

It is as wondrous a scene as any Hollywood screenwriter might invent. Reading this next section of Revelation, at first our mind's eye lights upon a white horse. Then our attention is drawn to the rider on the white horse. "His eyes are like blazing fire, and on his head are many crowns. . . . He is dressed in a robe dipped in blood, and his name is the Word of God. . . . Coming out of his mouth is a sharp sword with which to strike down the nations" (Revelation 19:12-15). This is the Lord Jesus Christ in the fullness of his divine majesty.

OPEN

List some ways earthly rulers typically display their power, and reflect on the purposes behind these exhibitions.

STUDY

"I saw heaven standing open," John writes (Revelation 19:11). The phrase alerts us to the fact that he is about to be given a special revelation of Christ and is going to share it with us. *Read Revelation 19:11-16.*

1. The names and the description of the rider on the white horse leave us with no doubt whatsoever that this is the Lord Jesus Christ in the fullness of his divine majesty. By what four names is he identified (vv. 11-13, 16)?

2. What do these four names of Christ tell you about him?

3. John wrote of the rider that "with justice he judges and wages war" (v. 11). What aspects of the rider's appearance show that he comes to judge with the justice of God?

4. What is the contrast between the robe of Christ (v. 13) and the robes of his armies of followers (v. 14)?

Summary: It is almost impossible to visualize the portrait of the Messiah that John describes—his eyes on fire, his head with many crowns, his mouth holding a sword, his hand brandishing a scepter while his feet are treading out grapes. Symbolically, however, it is a spectacular picture of the Lord Jesus Christ in majesty, power, authority, and justice, coming to destroy the powers of evil.

5. Following this revelation of Christ as the rider on the white horse, we would naturally expect him to ride forth to the last battle. In

anticipation of it and its casualties, an angel issues a loud and grim invitation. *Read Revelation 19:17-21.* What are the differences between "the great supper of God" (vv. 17-18) and "the wedding supper of the Lamb" already mentioned (Revelation 19:9)?

6. What is the outcome of the confrontation between Christ and his army versus the beast, the kings of the earth, and their armies?

So the dramatic moment has come. The two armies, divine and demonic, are facing one another. It is the threshold of Armageddon. What happens next? Nothing! It is a great anticlimax. For the truth is that the battle has already been fought and won on the cross and by the resurrection of Jesus.

Summary: Babylon has already been overthrown (Revelation 18). Now the two beasts will be destroyed (Revelation 19:20), leaving the dragon's fate until Revelation 20.

7. Revelation 19 concludes with the vision of the victorious rider on the white horse—in other words, with the end of history. We must not imagine, therefore, that Revelation 20 begins where chapter 19 leaves off. Having a *parallelist* understanding of the book, I believe that, yet again, John is recapitulating his story from the beginning. Within the fifteen verses of chapter 20 he retells the outline of church history between the first and second comings of Christ. *Read Revelation 20:1-6.* What is the purpose of Satan's confinement (v. 3)?

8. Who reigns with Christ during the thousand years (vv. 4-6)?

The expression "for a thousand years" occurs in Revelation 20:1-6 four times, on each occasion with a different reference. First, Satan is bound "for a thousand years" (v. 2). Second, the nations are no longer deceived "until the thousand years [are] ended" (v. 3). Third, the resurrected saints and martyrs reign with Christ "a thousand years" (v. 4). Fourth, the same resurrected ones serve God and Christ as priests "for a thousand years" (v. 6).

9. *Read Revelation 20:7-10.* The contours of the story are familiar. Already this army, marching to the battle of Armageddon, has been described three or four times (Revelation 11:18; 16:12-16; 19:19). Each time, as the two armies face each other, we expect a clash of arms, violence, and blood. What happens in this scenario (vv. 9-10)?

Summary: Each time there is no battle, for God himself intervenes and forestalls the conflict. Christ comes in person, the rider on the white horse, and overthrows the lawless one with the breath of his mouth (2 Thessalonians 1:7-10; 2:8). Or, as John puts it here, "fire came down from heaven and devoured them" (Revelation 20:9).

10. Now that the dragon, the two beasts, and the harlot have all been destroyed, all opposition to God's people (whether physical persecution, false ideology, or moral compromise) has disappeared with them, and the time has come for the judgment of individuals. *Read Revelation 20:11-15.* Who do you think is being judged at the great white throne and why?

11. Books are opened, both the many books recording the deeds of the dead and the single "book of life" registering those who belong to the Lamb (Revelation 3:5; 13:8). On what basis will judgment be made?

Summary: We sinners are justified by God's grace through faith in Christ alone. At the same time, we will be judged by our good works. The reason for this is that Judgment Day will be a public occasion, and good works will be the only visible evidence that can be produced to attest to the authenticity of our faith. "Faith by itself, if it is not accompanied by action, is dead" (James 2:17).

APPLY

How have you seen the power of Satan limited by God?

How has Christ showed himself "faithful and true" to you?

What difference does it make for you that the battle over evil has already been won by Christ's cross and resurrection?

PRAY

Pray that you will know the victory of Christ in every area where you struggle against sin. Pray for the assurance that you are ready to stand before God's throne.

THE BRIDEGROOM CLAIMS HIS BRIDE

REVELATION 21:1-22:5

Revelation 20 ended with the fearful contrast between those who are registered in the book of life and those who will experience the second death—that is, between life and death as the alternative destinies awaiting humankind. Revelation 21–22 also mentions the second death (Revelation 21:8), but the whole focus is on life—the book of life (Revelation 21:27), the water of life (Revelation 21:6; 22:1-2, 17), and the tree of life (Revelation 22:2, 14, 19). "Eternal life" means the personal knowledge of God through Jesus Christ (John 17:3), just as the second death means separation from him. John illustrates this life, the ultimate and glorious destiny of the people of God, by the use of three powerful metaphors in this next section of Revelation.

OPEN

When you think of the world in its present circumstances, what would you most like to see "made new" and why?

STUDY

The first eight verses of chapter 21 seem to celebrate the newness of God's eschatological work. They are variations on the theme of newness. *Read Revelation 21:1-8.*

1. How and from where does the new Jerusalem appear (v. 2)?

2. In what ways will the new heaven and new earth be different from the "old order of things" (vv. 3-4)?

3. What strikes you as the most radical change from the old to the new order?

4. How does the one on the throne declare his authority over life and death (vv. 5-8)?

It is important to affirm that our Christian hope looks forward not to an ethereal heaven but to a renewed universe, related to the present world by both continuity and discontinuity. Just as the individual Christian is a "new creation" in Christ (2 Corinthians 5:17), the same person but transformed, and just as the resurrection body will be the same body with its identity intact (remember Jesus' scars) yet invested with new powers, so the new heaven and the new earth will not be a replacement universe but a regenerated universe, purged of all present imperfection, with no more pain, sin, or death.

5. *Read Revelation 21:9-21.* At the beginning of this chapter, John saw the Holy City, the new Jerusalem, coming down beautifully dressed like a bride (Revelation 21:2). Now he is invited to see the bride but is shown the city (Revelation 21:10). It is obvious that the two metaphors illustrate the same truth. How does the city encompass both the Old and New Testaments (vv. 12, 14)?

6. How are the city's solidity and security expressed (vv. 12-17)?

7. How is the beauty of the city expressed (vv. 11, 18-21)?

Summary: The new Jerusalem is a massive, impregnable fortress, symbolizing the security and peace of the people of God. The presence of God permeates the whole city. It is not only huge and solid but also beautiful, shining with the glory of God and flashing with the brilliance of a very precious stone, perhaps a diamond.

8. *Read Revelation 21:22-27.* What is conspicuously absent from the new Jerusalem and why (v. 22)?

9. The readers of John's letter had only oil lamps for artificial light. What significance do you think they would find in the images of light in verses 23-25?

10. How do verses 26-27 demonstrate that the new Jerusalem will be a place of honor?

11. *Read Revelation 22:1-5.* We are still in the city, but we have left the walls, gates, and foundations, and the emphasis is on the river of life and the tree of life. These allusions alert us that John has the Garden of Eden in mind. What are some features of the water of life (vv. 1-2)?

12. What life-giving properties does the tree offer (v. 2)?

John has a remarkable facility for mixing his metaphors. He jumps abruptly from one to another—the city, the garden, and the wedding—without any apparent sense of incongruity. It is as difficult to visualize a city as a bride, or a bride as a city, as it is to visualize a lion as a lamb or a lamb as a lion. Nevertheless, it is not difficult to interpret the symbols. All three metaphors—the city, the garden, and the wedding—represent our close, personal fellowship with God, which begins now, once we have been reconciled to him, and which will be consummated when Christ comes.

13. How does John describe the closeness with God that the redeemed will enjoy (vv. 3-5)?

Summary: In the opening of this study, we saw that "eternal life" means the personal knowledge of God through Jesus Christ. John illustrates this life—the ultimate and glorious destiny of the people of God—by the use of three distinct metaphors. The first is security in the city of God, the new Jerusalem. The second is restored access to the tree of life in the Garden of Eden. The third is the intimate relationship of bride and bridegroom in marriage.

APPLY

In your everyday life, how real to you is the hope of this passage in Revelation?

How might your outlook on problems change if you saw them in the light of this secure hope?

Who else do you know who needs the hope of this passage?

PRAY

Thank God for the promise of the new Jerusalem, where we will live with God and where there will be no sin, pain, or death. Praise him that, in his love and mercy, he desires for us to be with him forever.

CHRIST PROMISING TO RETURN

The last sixteen verses of the book of Revelation are a kind of appendix or epilogue containing an assortment of warnings and exhortations. Three main themes stand out. *First*, John is concerned with authenticating his book and demonstrating its authority. *Second*, John issues his appeals and warnings against the background of anticipated judgment. *Third*, and the most distinctive feature of the passage, Jesus repeats the grand affirmation, "Look, I am coming soon!"

OPEN

Advertising and fundraising letters often include a special appeal in a PS. No doubt the letters have been revised several times before being printed, so why do you think they still include a PS at the end?

STUDY

1. *Read Revelation 22:6-11.* What did the angel tell John concerning the revelation John had received (vv. 6, 10-11)?

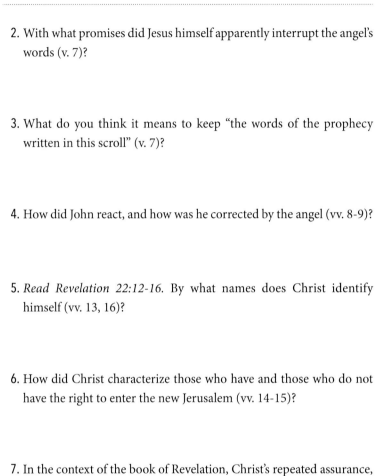

2. With what promises did Jesus himself apparently interrupt the angel's words (v. 7)?

3. What do you think it means to keep "the words of the prophecy written in this scroll" (v. 7)?

4. How did John react, and how was he corrected by the angel (vv. 8-9)?

5. *Read Revelation 22:12-16.* By what names does Christ identify himself (vv. 13, 16)?

6. How did Christ characterize those who have and those who do not have the right to enter the new Jerusalem (vv. 14-15)?

7. In the context of the book of Revelation, Christ's repeated assurance, "Look, I am coming soon," has a special significance. It indicates that, although he is coming to judge, he is also coming to complete the salvation of his people, coming as the heavenly bridegroom to claim his bride. *Read Revelation 22:17-21.* What mood prevails in this final passage of Revelation?

Three times in Revelation 22, Jesus declares that he is coming soon (vv. 7, 12, 20). How should we interpret the adverb *soon*? We need to remember that with the great events of Christ's coming, death, resurrection, and exaltation, the new age had dawned. There is now nothing on God's eschatological calendar before the parousia. The parousia is the very next event on his timetable.

Christian disciples are characterized by faith, hope, and love. Faith apprehends the *already* of Christ's achievement. Hope looks forward to the *not yet* of his salvation. And love characterizes our life *now* in the meantime. So, *soon* may be chronologically inexact, but it is theologically correct.

8. What longing and what promise are expressed in verse 17?

9. How does the Christian church today resemble a bride waiting for her bridegroom?

John has already declared that "the wedding of the Lamb has come," that "his bride has made herself ready," and that "those who are invited to the wedding supper of the Lamb" are blessed (Revelation 19:7, 9). Mixing metaphors, John has also described the new Jerusalem as "coming down out of heaven from God, prepared as a bride beautifully dressed for her husband" (Revelation 21:2, 9). But where is the bridegroom? He is nowhere to be seen! It is not for the bride to fetch the bridegroom but for the bridegroom to go and fetch his bride. She has made herself ready. Now, however, she can do no more than wait.

10. How does John affirm the authority of his book (vv. 18-19)?

11. After all that has gone before, does the ending of Revelation (vv. 20-21) surprise you, or does it seem to fit, and why?

Summary: The book of Revelation leaves the church waiting, hoping, expecting, longing, as the bride eagerly looking for her bridegroom, clinging to his threefold promise that he is coming soon, and encouraged by others who echo her call, "Amen. Come, Lord Jesus." Meanwhile, she is confident that his grace will be sufficient for her until the eternal wedding feast begins and she is united to her bridegroom forever.

APPLY

Do you eagerly join with the prayer of Revelation 22:20, "Come, Lord Jesus"? Or do you have misgivings, even fears, about Christ's coming?

Do your feelings even vary from day to day?

What certainty do you find in the final two chapters of Revelation to give you confidence for his coming?

How has this study of the book of Revelation affected your ideas about Jesus Christ?

How has this study of the book of Revelation affected your personal commitment to Christ?

PRAY

Thank the Lord for the sure promise of his return. Pray that you will live in expectation of his return, looking for him but not shirking in any way the work he has given you to do as you wait for him.

GUIDELINES FOR LEADERS

If leading a small group is something new for you, don't worry. These sessions are designed to be led easily. Because the Bible study questions flow from observation to interpretation to application, you may feel as if the studies lead themselves.

You don't need to be an expert on the Bible or a trained teacher to lead a small group discussion. As a leader, you can guide group members to discover for themselves what the Bible has to say and to listen for God's guidance. This method of learning will allow group members to remember much more of what is said than a lecture would.

This study guide is flexible. You can use it with a variety of groups—students, professionals, neighborhood, or church groups. Each study takes forty-five to sixty minutes in a group setting.

There are some important facts to know about group dynamics and encouraging discussion. The following suggestions should equip you to effectively and enjoyably fulfill your role as leader.

PREPARING FOR THE STUDY

1. Ask God to help you understand and apply the passage in your own life. Unless this happens, you will not be prepared to lead others. Pray, too, for the various members of the group. Ask God to open your hearts to the message of his Word and motivate you to action.

2. Read the introduction to the entire guide to get an overview of the topics that will be explored.

3. As you begin each study, read and reread the assigned Bible passage to familiarize yourself with it.

4. This study guide is based on the New International Version of the Bible. It will help you and the group if you use this translation as the basis for your study and discussion. The New Revised Standard Version is also recommended.

5. Carefully work through each question in the study. Spend time in meditation and reflection as you consider how to respond.

6. Write your thoughts and responses in the space provided in the study guide. This will help you to express your understanding of the passage clearly.

7. It may help to have a Bible dictionary handy. Use it to look up any unfamiliar words, names, or places. (For additional help on how to study a passage, see *How to Lead a LifeGuide Bible Study* from Inter-Varsity Press, USA.)

8. Take the "Apply" portion of each study seriously. Consider how you need to apply the Scripture to your life. Remember that the group members will follow your lead in responding to the studies. They will not go any deeper than you do.

LEADING THE STUDY

1. Begin the study on time. Open with prayer, asking God to help the group to understand and apply the passage.

2. Be sure that everyone in your group has a study guide. Encourage the group to prepare beforehand for each discussion by reading the introduction to the guide and by working through the questions in each study.

3. At the beginning of your first time together, explain that these studies are meant to be discussions, not lectures. Encourage the members of the group to participate. However, do not put pressure on those who may be hesitant to speak during the first few sessions.

4. Have a group member read aloud the introduction at the beginning of the discussion.

5. Every session begins with an "open" question, which is meant to be asked before the passage is read. These questions are designed to introduce the theme of the study and encourage group members to begin to open up. Encourage as many members as possible to participate, and be ready to get the discussion going with your own response. These opening questions can reveal where our thoughts or feelings need to be transformed by Scripture. That is why it is especially important not to read the passage before the question is asked. The passage will tend to color the honest reactions people would otherwise give because they are, of course, supposed to think the way the Bible does.

6. Have a group member read aloud the passage to be studied.

7. As you ask the study questions, keep in mind that they are designed to be used just as they are written. You may simply read them aloud. Or you may prefer to express them in your own words.

There may be times when it is appropriate to deviate from the study guide. For example, a question may have already been answered. If so, move on to the next question. Or someone may raise an important question not covered in the guide. Take time to discuss it, but try to keep the group from going on tangents.

8. Avoid answering your own questions. If necessary, repeat or rephrase them until they are clearly understood. Or point the group to the commentary woven into the guide to clarify the context or meaning *without answering the question*. An eager group quickly becomes passive and silent if members think the leader will do most of the talking.

9. Don't be afraid of silence in response to the discussion questions. People may need time to think about the question before formulating their answers.

10. Don't be content with just one answer. Ask, "What do the rest of you think?" or "Anything else?" until several people have given answers to the question.

11. Acknowledge all contributions. Try to be affirming whenever possible. Never reject an answer. If it is clearly off-base, ask, "Which verse led you to that conclusion?" or again, "What do the rest of you think?"

12. Don't expect every answer to be addressed to you, even though this will probably happen at first. As group members become more at ease, they will begin to truly interact with each other. This is one sign of healthy discussion.

13. Don't be afraid of controversy. It can be very stimulating. If you don't resolve an issue completely, don't be frustrated. Explain that the group will move on and God may enlighten all of you in later sessions.

14. Periodically summarize what the group has said about the passage. This helps to draw together the various ideas mentioned and gives continuity to the study. But don't preach.

15. Conclude your time together with conversational prayer, adapting the prayer suggestion at the end of the study to your group. Ask for God's help in following through on the commitments you've made.

16. End on time.

Many more suggestions and helps can be found in *How to Lead a Life-Guide Bible Study* and *The Big Book on Small Groups* (both from Inter-Varsity Press, USA) or *Housegroups* (Crossway Books, UK). Reading through one of these books would be worth your time.

ALSO AVAILABLE

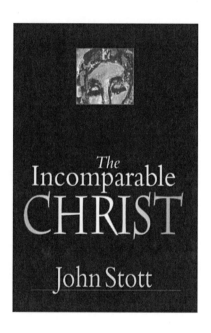